chop 1

chop

a collection of kwansabas for fannie lou hamer

treasure shields redmond

co-winner of the Rustbelt Appa/Afrilachian
Midwest chapbook contest
chop, a collection of kwansabas for fannie lou
hamer

ISBN :9781546832119

Original Cover Art by FrankD Robinson

Author Photo by Kim Love

chop 3

Chop

a collection of kwansabas for fannie lou
hamer

Dedication

Yaa Asantewa Williams
a free woman of color

&

Eugene B. Redmond
Ark/eye/tech of the kwansaba

Acknowledgements

"around the time of medgar", "jericho" and "from my parlor window, 1964". *e Sou'wester 39.2.* (Spring, 2011) 30-32

"October 16, 1917, Montgomery County, Mississippi", "makn ends meet" and "chop". *Sententia 4.* (Winter, 2012) 122-124

TABLE OF CONTENT

Who was Fannie Lou Hamer?

When one thinks of the millions of souls lost during the transatlantic slave trade, the missed potential immediately jumps to mind. All genocide robs us of the few geniuses that each culture produces. At the beginning of the previous century the pernicious system named Jim Crow served as another sort of genocide in the U.S. A genocide of potential. Many scholars have written of the number of lynchings during Jim Crow, perhaps the most famous one being Ida B. Wells's A Red Record. Along with the incomprehensible loss of life, however, are the people who lived, but not really. e ones who weren't fortunate enough to die. Those who lived believing a system that counted them as less valuable, less competent, less human; that this system was right, godly, and, (maybe worst of all), unchangeable. When young people from the Student Nonviolent Coordinating Committee walked across a cotton field in 1962 they didn't know they were about to ignite

one of the greatest intellects of the 20th century. Fannie Lou Hamer was born in 1917 in Sunflower county. She was a black woman. She was her mother's 20th child. The first half of her life was lived quite unremarkably. She was a churchgoing woman who married, raised two daughters, and through pure savvy and hard work, rose to the rank

of timekeeper on her plantation. Mrs. Hamer joined the movement for civil rights without so much as a second thought, at the age of 44. She was known to reply to those who thought she should worry about being killed, that "[Jim Crow] had been killing [her] a little bit everyday" [of her life]. Mrs. Hamer went on to challenge the sitting Democratic Party in Mississippi, to run for numerous offices, to become a valued member of Martin Luther King's cadre of movement soldiers, to offer her very beaten body as evidence that Jim Crow had tried but not succeeded in killing her most radical self. These poems are my love letter to Mrs. Hamer, and every black woman like her who raised me in Mississippi, and who, for me, were not exceptional. With these poems I am exposing to the world, in much the same way the young people from SNCC did, that genocide is overwhelming, but it is not total. Beneath the shrapnel of Jim Crow lay undetonated intellects --working, serving, and keeping time, until they explode.

october 16, 1917, montgomery county, mississippi

boss say i birthd twenty field hands
then givd me fifty dollars for fannie.
done promise this last one to god.
dream i givd her to the priest.
took her behind the holy of holies,
came out full grown and singn glory.
shook me woke. knowd i been changd.

makn ends meet

juke joint aint church; though prayr savd

me and paps from plain greens, flour

gravy, pig's ears, feet, snout. blues aint

christ-like til they fill bellies burstn

with home brew, moon shin'n through mason

jars like gold teeth against black lips,

greasd. skillets testify: faith fries, with work.

chop

yam on stove, water jug ready, spicket

bath, rag tied. groggy hands can't be

no stumbln block. nor suckln babe to

tend. sun be waitn his turn, watchn

me beat him to field. cotton is

calln. if five hundred pounds mean a

bale, how negroes be called "no count"?

ears and fingers

aint babies' ears and fingers sweet? bare

foot winters harden they feet; ashy elbows,

and scabbed knees grow callous. not them

ears and fingers. pretty fat thumbs, lobes

with baby hair still on 'em. mobs

even crave 'em. pickld tokns, floatn cute

 as can be in big store windows.

redish'

bus bound for indianola, full with colord

bodies. cotton choppd heads full with freedom

lessons. "be polite. eye contact. talk up."

we aint wrong. we just know better.

extra shoes and my own freedom pen.

we gon' redish today. gon' redish today.

gon' redish today. we gon' redish today.

boss say she can come back

marlowe say: *she can come back, just*

take her name off that voter roll.

back to field. back to cabin. *back*

slidn is a sin, i say. back

to slopjar. back to thinkn rights was

flies -- been shoo'n them when i shouldv

been invitn them home for freedom supper.

poll tax

weren't right how they did us. wouldn't

kick no dog that ain't barkn. hell,

i was 44. told that doctor 34.

auntie, we just gone make it so

you don't be bothered with eve's curse,

he say. i votes for them babies.

babies that won't never stand in line.

around the time of medgar

first beatn was in a hot winona
jail. corn whiskey paid to a colord
man. beat me till he give out.
beat me like they told him. beat
my hips for bein' wide, my back
for not being bent. they beat us
all for the look in our eyes.

favorite verse

"whose hatred is covered by deceit, his wickedness
shall be showed before the whole congregation."
proverbs 26:26

script and verse i told the jailer's
wife. she bring lunch for her man.
i tell her bread of life hath
made one blood. her man drew blood,
do dirt behind bars. proverbs prove it
will come to light. " i been born
again", she say. lady, *read* your bible.

justice

we stay in holly springs. can't stay

in oxford. awaitn trial like daniel. den

so loud we hear it 25 miles

away. sheriff, police, highway patrol namd law

breakr. they got cousins in the jury

box, show'n they lion teeth; eyes shut

tight to this little light of mine.

white or colord

young folks argue into dawn bout whether

whites can work down here along side

colord . i done washd, cookd, caught they

babies. always behind or below. nevr beside.

my body broke for three days over

this debt. the spirit makes me ask:

aint it time they shared this cup?

my part

between kennedy and four little girls lay

mississippi. between texas sniper and georgia terror

stretch delta dust. wedged inside history. mingld

in medgar's bloody carport. i stand ready

to fall five foot four inches into

freedom. cock's crow won't signal denial out

my mouth. i'll take up the cross.

freedom summer

i prepare them best i can. tell

about the white man's deep fear; afraid

of payback cause he deserve it. we

need their bodies. young bodies from good

 homes -- white bodies -- the kind folks can't

stand to see broken. israel done come

out of egypt. freedom summer done come.

from my parlor window, 1964

hate throw'n water on their fire. white

and colord holdn hands, going to town.

their clear eyes show me what could

be. see 'em under my pecan tree?

pointn at clouds, elbows touchn. shamed folks

into livn like the christ they claim.

do they daddies know they *this* free?

pap's blues

black balled is how they call it.

any colord redish', subject to get put

off the land. these crackers won't give

a crippld crab a crutch. now martin

king send a check every month. freedom

is fannie's trade. i aint got to

work. so i work on this bourbon.

jericho

johnson calld me "ignornt". while he can't

see what's wrong in mississippi. then throw

a party, where half the childrn aint

invitd. the word say: my mansion is

in heaven. but before i get there

we might march around 'lantic city 7

times. bring a white house tumbln down.

is this america?

they call it a hear'n, but don't

nobody listen. too busy tryn to dickr

with the devil. i tell 'em what

god loves. see tears in they eyes.

what is they cryn for? colord done

cried an ocean. prayd enough to fill

a bible. now we want freedom. now.

3 ways til sunday

fannie, annie and vickie, three ways til
sunday. vickie hailing from forrest county. annie
raisd in madison. bear'n empty tomb witness
2000 years later. we roll away stone
for america. show 'em what's missing. i
loves these women. they accept my coarse
cloth. make a coat of many colors.

not be moved

we didn't come all this way for
no two seats. we make our stand
here on the old side of the
country. we saw these shores first. now
we come full circle. show you our
tree roots. shall not be moved. shall
over come. bent but not brokn. amen.

guinea, west africa – 1964

blacker than the tar i was always

 told they would boil me in. i

was caught up in toure's white robe

like we gon' be caught on jubilee

day. he kissd me on both jaws!

put a ring on my prodigl hands.

 now can you imagn johnson doin that?

malcolm

heard me sing freedom; tell about marlowe

kickn me off the job; about winona

jail. mr. x, with his red self,

preached white folk's funeral; eye for eye

and they sittn in the front row.

said he didn't feel like a man

when he heard how they beat me.

hard hearted

not when your rivers turnd bloody; not
when mlk's truth thundrd; not even when
your son fell in texas. now we
frog jumpn through your red dc. got
us a "moses" and a "aaron". couldn't
stop now if we wanted to. freedom
like fire shut up in my bones.

mississippi

is a hoish man on the porch.
4 am -- smelln like slave quartrs and
juke smoke. sweet talkn his way back
in the union with oaths he nevr
plans to keep. then talk shit when
you remind him, sayn: *you knew who
i was when you opend the door.*

isaiah 38:1

in 1882 the last colord rump sat

here on this capitol floor. now 3

black women come to clean house; droppd

from america's lap, weand on fire, teeth

cut on lynch rope. our wheat straw

truth can not be denied. thus saith

the lord: set thine house in order.

preachers

chickn eatn preachrs. tom fool colords. we
have to watch them. this fire done
caught hold. tend to it like your
field. we all eat off what grows
here. can't have no coon stealn tendr
plants before they time. we almost there.
just keep your hand to the plow.

head start

po childrn don't see nobody like them
in the pre primer. see dick eat
dirt? see jane chop cotton? look at
jane's feet. do she cut the toe
off her shoes when they get too
small? do her hands crave a pencil
but make do with a dull stick?

vietnam

*"If this is a GREAT SOCIETY I'd hate to see a
bad one"*

some get live sons back. some get
dead flags, tucked tight as a preachr's
grip. live ones come home full of
hell; wasted minds mostly still over seas.
what i could do with them soldiers
in sunflower county. how shall we sing
the lord's songs in a strange land?

paris green

poison put in my daddy's trough killd

our cow dead as a preachr in

memphs. murdrd our mule with paris green

envy ugly as 3 lynchd boys. here

lately the mob looks like us. stirrd

up in our food till we can't

tell what's good from what is poison.

little member

the word say this little tongue can

make big trouble. i use simple words:

free, land, free, medicne. they push back

with big words: marxist, social, exprmnt. just

one little woman talkn, will raise cain.

never met karl marx, but i know

a good idea when i hear one.

bound

my man paps wants to save me

up like change but this thick black

body is spent. spare breast. spare kidney,

fibrous womb taken fore i knowd it

was. gone lay down my burden. i'm

river side bound for the promise, god

i would serve him till i die.

Why the Kwansaba?

I chose the Kwansaba through which to channel Mississippi's proto- womanist Black activist/organizer, Fannie Lou Hamer because the brevity of the form mirrors the shots of bourbon strong imagery that I hoped to convey. Each poem pushes forward an "aint it the truth" moment from the perspective of Hamer, and some of the other family members who witnessed her genius. e form, created by poet Eugene B. Redmond is "In general . . . a praise song to a person, a principle, or an event". Even though it is true that the poems "praise" Hamer's accomplishments, they aspire to do much more. ey also collude with the seven lines/seven words stricture in order to give homage to Hamer's southern charismatic Christianity (the same sort in which

I was raised) that says "seven is God's favorite number". Finally, like many of Dickenson's masterpieces or Berryman's Dream Songs the poems seek to work in concert using the economical nature of the Kwansaba form to get at what was most essential about Hamer's mammoth contribution to American life.

About the Author

A Mississippi native, Treasure Shields Redmond is a poet, speaker, diversity and inclusion coach, and social justice educator. In 2016 she founded her company, Feminine Pronoun Consultants, LLC. Even though Treasure is completing a PhD in English Literature and Criticism, is a published writer, gifted veteran educator, and has spoken on stages all over the U.S. and in Europe, she uses her humble beginnings in the federal housing projects in Meridian, Mississippi to fuel her passion for helping college-bound families navigate college admissions painlessly and profitably, and offering perceptive leaders creative diversity and inclusion facilitation. Additional information on her poetry, writing, and multidimensional practice are available at: www.FemininePronoun.com.

chop 43

CPSIA information can be obtained
at www.ICGtesting.com
Printed in the USA
LVHW081048290321
682819LV00014B/387